Thirsk

a historic town in the
Vale of Mowbray

Albion
Press

PREFACE

Writing this brief account of Thirsk's history has been an enjoyable and challenging experience. Inevitably, I have only skimmed the surface of the town's past and some themes are thus dealt with in a cursory manner or are not mentioned at all. Nevertheless, I hope that the text is an engaging and informative outline of Thirsk's story and that it will stimulate people to delve deeper into a fascinating subject.

Glen Lyndon Dodds
Sunderland
16 September 2018

Opposite: Pudding Pie Hill

FROM PREHISTORIC TO STUART TIMES

Thirsk is an attractive market town and lies in the Vale of Mowbray, an expanse of generally flat terrain between the North York Moors and the Pennines that has attracted human activity for countless generations. For example, items dating from the Bronze Age (c.2,250-c.800 BC) have been uncovered in the Station Road area of Thirsk. However, the most notable relic of the neighbourhood's prehistory is the burial mound called Pudding Pie Hill which may date from the early Bronze Age. This substantial barrow lies close to the east bank of the Cod Beck on the southeastern outskirts of Sowerby and a stone's throw south of Blakey Lane.

Like many other barrows up and down the country, Pudding Pie Hill was reused as a place to inter the dead centuries later, for Victorian excavators discovered three Anglian interments in the mound. The Angles were a Germanic people from northern Germany and southern Denmark who became the dominant figures in Yorkshire in the 6th century AD and their language, Old English, supplanted the Celtic tongue. In addition, 10 graves dating from the first half of that century

were uncovered during excavations in the mid 1990s on Castle Garth near the heart of Thirsk. In the 9th century, moreover, other Germanic people, Vikings from Denmark, arrived and it is sometimes said that Thirsk's name is of Danish origin and derives from a word meaning lake or fen.

At the time of Domesday Book in 1086, the dominant figure in Thirsk (which was then spelt 'Tresche') was Hugh FitzBaldric, a baron who held extensive estates in Yorkshire and in the Midlands—his property in Yorkshire alone numbered around 50 manors. But shortly thereafter, the bulk of Hugh's property in Yorkshire, passed into the hands of Robert de Stuteville who is thought to have erected a motte and bailey castle, the characteristic stronghold of the Norman era, at Thirsk in around 1092. The castle, sometimes wrongly said to have been pre-Conquest, occupied fairly level ground between today's Market Place and Newsham Road. One can still see part of the bailey (an enclosure) and surviving earthworks, including the western rampart and its outer ditch. To the east, the bailey was separated by a wide ditch from the motte—a mound presumably surmounted by a timber palisade and enclosing a wooden tower—and the summit of the motte is now partly occupied by a late Victorian house named Castle Villa. In addition, timber defences would have run along the top of the rampart enclosing the bailey.

Robert de Stuteville (who is sometimes incorrectly said to have later become known as Robert de Mowbray) experienced an abrupt change of fortune. In 1106 he was captured at the Battle of Tinchebrai in Normandy while fighting on behalf of Robert, Duke of Normandy, the elder brother and rival of England's king, Henry I. Stuteville's estates were thus seized by Henry who proceeded to reward one of his own household knights, a Norman called Nigel d'Aubigny, with much of the confiscated property, including Thirsk. Furthermore, the king granted Nigel land elsewhere in England, such as in Leicestershire and North-amptonshire. But that was not all. Henry also gave Nigel estates in Normandy previously forfeit by Robert de Mowbray, the Earl of North-umbria, who had lost his lands and liberty following an unsuccessful rebellion in 1095. Hence Nigel, a younger son of a minor Norman

Opposite: The earthworks of Thirsk Castle

landed family, became an important member of the Anglo-Norman baronage.

Nigel married twice. The first marriage, to the former wife of Robert de Mowbray, was childless but Nigel's second wife Gundreda gave him a son, Roger, who was born in around 1120 and was therefore under age when his father died in Normandy in 1129.

Just under a decade later, Roger fought against the Scots at the Battle of the Standard near Northallerton in 1138 (the English army had marched through Thirsk en route to confront the enemy) and, at around the same time, he changed his name to Roger de Mowbray. Moreover, in early 1141 he was one of the barons captured beside King Stephen at the Battle of Lincoln during a civil war known to history as the Anarchy.

During Roger's lifetime the number of monasteries in England grew rapidly and he played a role in this phenomenon. In 1145, for example, he established Newburgh Priory, a house for Augustinian canons located about nine miles southeast of Thirsk. Mowbray gave the canons an endowment that included property at Thirsk, most notably the parish church, St Mary's, which would thus be a source of revenue for the canons from tithes etc.

The parish was large (a common feature of parishes in the North of England) and included the neighbouring villages of Sowerby, Carlton Miniott and Sandhutton and each of these had a dependent chapel, although when they were built is unclear. At Sowerby, about half a mile south of Thirsk, the chapel was dedicated to St Oswald and the building, which now mostly dates from the 19th and 20th centuries and has become a parish church in its own right, contains fabric of Norman date, including the southwest doorway with its characteristic round head.

At some point before 1145, Thirsk was granted the status of a borough and held a weekly market. Evidently, the borough was a settlement on the east bank of the Cod Beck, a community that developed beside the York to Yarm road. It was here too, that a chapel dedicated to St James was constructed. The building is mentioned in the foundation charter of Newburgh Priory—the chapel was part of the priory's endowment— and Mowbray also granted the canons of Newburgh the right to buy and sell at Thirsk market without paying tolls and stallage.

The Norman doorway of St Oswald's

Sooner or later, the market shifted from 'Old Thirsk', as it became known, across a ford to 'New Thirsk' on the west bank of the stream. Here, a settlement, referred to as a 'vill' in 1145, had developed beside the castle and ultimately became the main focal point of activity.

Roger de Mowbray also played a role in events that led to the founding of one of England's greatest monasteries, Byland Abbey. In the late 1130s a small band of monks from the North West of England, whose monastery had just been destroyed by Scottish raiders, entered Yorkshire to seek help from Archbishop Thurstan of York, a well-known patron of monasticism. Exactly what followed is unclear for two versions of events were recorded in the late 12th century. One states that the monks were well received by Thurstan who sent them to Roger, and he, in turn, sent them to Hood (on the fringe of the North York Moors a short distance east of Thirsk) where one of his kinsmen was living as a hermit. The alternative account, though, says that the displaced monks arrived at Thirsk while en route to see Thurstan and here, by chance, were met by Roger's steward, an important official who decided to take the dejected monks to the castle. As they approached the stronghold, Roger's mother Gundreda caught sight of them from a high window and felt pity for the refugees whom she took under her wing and sent to her relative at Hood.

What is certain is that Roger de Mowbray provided the displaced monks with land at Hood and both he and his mother continued to support them in subsequent years. For example, Hood was not a suitable site for the monastic community to expand and so in the early 1140s the monks moved to Byland on the North York Moors, a location granted to them by Gundreda. Two more changes of location ensued, nonetheless, and the final move was completed in 1177 when the monks, who retained the name of Byland for their relocated monastery, settled around nine miles or so southeast of Thirsk and the majestic ruins of their Cistercian abbey still dominate the local landscape.

Meanwhile, in the years 1173-4 Roger was one of the numerous barons who rebelled against King Henry II and so Thirsk Castle was a rebel stronghold. But in 1174 the rebellion collapsed and Mowbray travelled to Northampton and offered his submission to the king, who

proceeded to have Thirsk Castle demolished two years later. Epworth in the Isle of Axholme (part of northern Lincolnshire) became the principal residence of the Mowbrays. Nevertheless, Thirsk remained part of their extensive network of property.

In the mid 1180s Roger travelled to the Holy Land to help defend Jerusalem from the infidels and was captured at the epic Battle of Hattin in July 1187, a defeat that sent shock waves through the Christian world and resulted in the seizure of Jerusalem by the Islamic leader, Saladin. Mowbray was soon ransomed and released but died in around 1188 and his place of burial is uncertain.[1]

At the beginning of the 13th century, Roger's grandson William granted a mill and land at Norby, on the northern outskirts of Thirsk, to a certain 'Philip, son of John.' In connection with this grant, the *Victoria History of the County of York* states: 'The mill was probably of considerable antiquity, for the island formed by the millrace and Cod Beck was granted by Roger de Mowbray to Newburgh Priory in 1145 and had previously been held by Richard the Priest.'

Not surprisingly, in view of his high status, William de Mowbray played a role on the national stage. Indeed, he was one of the barons who forced King John to sign Magna Carta (a charter of liberties) in June 1215. A civil war ensued and in the closing days of the year the king marched north against his enemies and some places were ransacked or burnt. Other centres of population, as Austin Lane Poole notes in *From Domesday Book to Magna Carta*, bought the king's goodwill for large sums of money to avoid destruction. This was true, for instance, of York and Beverley and Thirsk did likewise. It paid 80 marks to be spared from being set alight.[2]

Inevitably, in view of Thirsk's position on one of the country's major thoroughfares, the Great North Road—which passed between the

---

1   In an article published by the Haskins Society, John Gillingham aptly comments: 'Few English crusaders were as enthusiastic as Roger de Mowbray. He went on Crusade in 1147. According to John of Hexham, he won fame in single combat against a pagan commander. He almost certainly went on crusade again in 1177. And he undoubtedly went again in the 1180s.'

2   The civil war ended in 1217 in the reign of John's young son Henry III, and Mowbray died in or around 1224 and was buried at Newburgh Priory.

Opposite: Byland Abbey

castle and the marketplace and ran northward to Northallerton etc and southward to Topcliffe and beyond—several kings passed through the town or spent time here over the centuries. For example, Henry III was in Thirsk in 1227 and his son and successor Edward I travelled through the town in the years around 1300, including a stay of three days in 1296. Coincidentally, the borough had sent two MPs to parliament for the first time the previous year.

Kirkgate, one of Thirsk's main streets, was formerly part of this important highway and the parish church of St Mary, standing on an elevated position overlooking the road, must have caught the eye of many of the travellers wending their way along the road. For some people, however, this part of the town had less appeal for the manorial prison was located near the west end of the church. Reportedly, in the 13th century a number of prisoners escaped by bribing the bailiff, a state of affairs that understandably led to complaints.

During the 13th century the Mowbrays had a manor house on the site of their former castle. Overall, this was a peaceful era for the people of Thirsk but in the early decades of the 14th century their lives were affected by Scottish raids, for incursions from north of the border caused widespread fear and misery in Yorkshire. In 1316, for instance, the monks of Whitby Abbey lamented that their supply of 'corn and victuals' had suffered partly as a result of 'the frequent inroads of the Scots.' Raiders also made their presence directly felt at Thirsk for in 1322 Scots are said to have destroyed the manor house and associated dovecotes which, apparently, would henceforth remain in a desolate state. Moreover, in his thesis *Sacred Space*, Anthony Masinton has suggested that the parish church was damaged by the raiders and points to evidence that repair work ensued.

In 1322 John de Mowbray, whose extensive estates included Thirsk, took part in a rebellion against England's weak and ineffectual king, Edward II. The revolt was crushed by one of the monarch's able lieutenants who defeated the rebels at the Battle of Boroughbridge and Mowbray, who was in his late thirties, was hauled off to York where he was soon hanged. His estates were forfeit to the Crown and his wife and young son were imprisoned in the Tower of London. The family's

Opposite: The imposing St Mary's Church

downfall was reversed after Edward II's death in 1327 and so Thirsk returned into the hands of the Mowbrays.

As noted, a weekly market was held in Thirsk. Additional hustle and bustle was created by fairs, much more exciting and larger events. In 1293, for example, it was recorded that there was a three-day fair associated with the feast of St Felix of Nola (14 January), and in 1327 fairs were held on the Feasts of St James (25 July) and St Luke (18 October).

The most significant event that occurred in Thirsk during the late Middle Ages was the rebuilding of St Mary's Church in the popular Perpendicular style, the final phase of Gothic architecture—some of the previous church was retained during this process, as was true of part of the eastern wall of the tower. The task of rebuilding St Mary's is sometimes said to have happened in the years 1430-80 but a different chronology has been proposed by Anthony Masinton. He suggests, among other things, that the aisles of the nave may have been built between 1395 and 1429 and that the 'church was, in terms of the interior space,

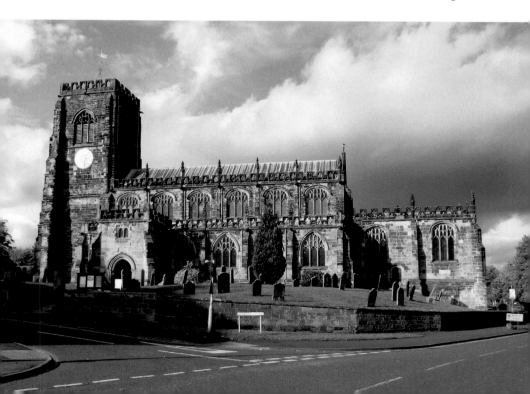

finished after the arcades, clerestory and chancel were completed by c.1460 at the latest, based on the heraldic evidence of the glass.' Finally, in the first half of the 16th century, the tower, whose lower stages had already been largely reconstructed during the rebuilding programme, was gradually raised to its present height of 80ft.

Of St Mary's, G.A. Poole comments: 'Taken as a whole, few Churches can be said to equal that of Thirsk, whether we consider its size, or its correctness of architectural detail.' For his part, the eminent architectural historian Sir Nikolaus Pevsner has aptly commented that St Mary's is unquestionably 'the most spectacular' Perpendicular church in the North Riding of Yorkshire.

The church is entered through an imposing porch and above the entrance passage is a room that housed a hermit, Thomas Parkinson, in the early 16th century. The porch opens to the nave (the 15th-century wooden door survives and is ornamented with traceried panels) and the spacious and well-lit nave has lofty arches opening to the aisles and is covered by an impressive timber ceiling which Masinton comments is 'arguably the finest timber roof in the Riding.'

The chancel—the east end of the church—is narrower than the rest of the building and has no aisles. In line with common practice, the rebuilding of this part of the church was likely funded by the canons of Newburgh Priory, to whom St Mary's had been granted in 1145. The chancel arch, though, dates from a programme of restoration in the 19th century. So that the chancel would be at the same level as the nave (the ground falls away at this point) it was built over a crypt which evidently was used as a vestry but may well have also been used as a schoolroom too.[1]

John, the 16th Lord Mowbray, died in 1476. He left a daughter who likewise went to her grave shortly thereafter. Consequently, Thirsk

---

1   In her account of Thirsk's history, M. Weston notes the existence of a school at Thirsk as early as 1396. In addition, Masinton observes: 'It seems that one of the chaplains of the St. Anne chantry [located within the church] also acted as schoolmaster c1436, if the numerous bequests of small amounts of money which he gave to children in the town can be interpreted as his students.' In 1546, moreover, a school was the responsibility of the Gild of the Blessed Mary in the Porch—a body linked to the church's porch—and the gild may have already run the school for a long time.

The church viewed from the nave

passed into the hands of William, Lord Berkeley, whose mother had been a Mowbray. Following his death in 1492 during the reign of Henry VII (the first of the Tudor monarchs) the manor of Thirsk passed into the hands of the Stanley family, Earls of Derby.

In the latter half of the 1530s, Henry VIII's government began closing abbeys and priories—an event known to history as the Dissolution of the Monasteries—and as a result Newburgh Priory's links with Thirsk came to an end for the priory was shut down in 1539 and the property passed into lay hands.

Subsequently, in 1559 (shortly after Elizabeth I ascended the throne) Catholicism was supplanted as the state religion by the Church of England. Some members of the clergy and their flocks were enthusiastic Protestants but others harboured a fondness for Catholic doctrine and ritual, a state of affairs that persisted. Hence, of Thirsk late in Elizabeth's reign, Masinton comments: 'Attachment to the old ways was still strong in the parish, as the reference to "popish vestments" at Thirsk in an entry in the Archiepiscopal Visitation Court book for 1586 makes clear.'

Turning to other matters, in late 1547 Thirsk had sent two MPs to Westminster for the first parliament of Edward VI. The borough had only done so once before (in 1295) but from now on Thirsk continued to have its own parliamentary representation. Among the early MPs was Christopher Lascelles, who was elected in November 1554 and retained the seat until 1559. He had strong local connections, for his family were the long-established lords of the manor of Sowerby and had held land in that village since the 12th century.

Henry Belasyse (an alternative spelling is 'Bellasis'), the son of a Yorkshire country gentleman, likewise served as an MP. He first became an MP for Thirsk in 1586 when he was in his early 30s and continued to represent the town until 1597. Furthermore, he did so again in the years 1601-04 and in the latter year succeeded to his father's estate, Newburgh Priory. Henry's son and grandson were also MPs for Thirsk and the family thus largely dominated the constituency over many years.

In 1628 another country gentleman, William Frankland of Great Thirkleby (just over four miles southeast of Thirsk), was elected to serve as one of the constituency's MPs. The following year, however, Charles I dissolved parliament and it only reassembled in 1640 when Frankland was re-elected to sit in what became known as the 'Short Parliament' and he died later that year.

In 1642, the year which saw the commencement of the English Civil War, the Cod Beck was described as the 'Broad Beck leading to Thirske'. Nowadays, the volume of water carried by the stream is less than was the case in previous generations partly as a result of the construction of the Cod Beck Reservoir above Osmotherley in the mid 20th century.

The Civil War led to the trial and execution of the king in 1649, and England became a republic in which Puritans held sway. In 1660, however, shortly after the death of Oliver Cromwell, the monarchy was restored when Charles II returned from exile. Moreover, the Church of England, which had been abolished by the victors of the war, was re-established in 1662 and under legislation passed that year, members of the clergy were obliged to take an oath that they would adhere to the teachings and liturgy of the restored Church. Over 2,000 refused to do so nationwide and Matthew Hill, the Cambridge-educated curate of Thirsk parish church, was one of those who failed to comply. He was therefore ejected from his living and moved to York where, at risk to himself, he preached privately in the city for a short time before sailing to Maryland in North America.

By 1662 a new religious denomination, the Quakers—who initially called themselves the Seekers—had come into existence and in 1647 Thomas Pratt had bought a dwelling in Kirkgate to serve as a meeting place. Quakers soon made enemies by, for example, refusing to remove their hats when in the presence of people of higher social rank, and by sometimes disrupting church services by hectoring members of the clergy. Not surprisingly, they were thus persecuted. Among other

A weeping willow beside Cod Beck

things, the Five-Mile Act of 1665 forbade them (and other dissenters) to congregate within five miles of towns and so Thirsk's Quakers met elsewhere such as at Kilburn, a village about 6 miles to the southeast. Members of the local Quaker community included Brian Peart and, as John Woods has noted, he was evidently prosperous because he had to pay tax for six hearths in Thirsk in 1673 at a time when the vast majority of houses only had one or two hearths. Although Quakers continued to face some animosity, their position became easier as a result of the Act of Toleration passed in 1689.

Meanwhile, in 1667 a property in Kirkgate had been conveyed to the Lord Lieutenant of the North Riding, Thomas Belasyse, the second Viscount Fauconberg. The building was to serve as a house of correction, that is, a place where vagrants and other down and outs were compelled to work.

Moreover, in line with the Poor Relief Act of 1662, steps were taken to stop labourers from elsewhere settling in the parish in case they fell on hard times and would require support. To cite an instance, on 11 July 1671 it was recorded that the constables of Thirsk were authorised to apprehend a labourer and his wife and take them to Sessay. If the couple proved defiant and resisted their removal, or returned to Thirsk after being taken to Sessay, they were to be arrested and detained in the House of Correction and there, as a contemporary document (quoted by Eleanor Trotter in her book, *Seventeenth Century Life in the Country Parish*) says, 'dealt withall as stubborn, contemptuous disobeyers of this Court, there to be detained until they shall give security to a J.P. that they shall and will, within two days of such security, repair to Seazey and there remain … and be no further troublesome to the inhabitants of Thirske.'

Inevitably, from time to time bequests were made for charitable purposes. For instance, in his will of 10 November 1692 Joseph Midgeley, who held the living of St Oswald's in Sowerby, granted the modest annual sum of 15 shillings to charity. The money was to come from an enclosure called Bransby Croft and was collected for generations and a parliamentary report of 1820 notes that it was then paid by Thirsk's lord of the manor, John Bell, who owned the relevant tract of land.

Opposite: Thirsk Hall

THIRSK IN GEORGIAN & VICTORIAN TIMES

The Bell family became lords of the manor in 1723 when Ralph Bell of Sowerby, who had served as a member of parliament for Thirsk from 1710 to 1717, bought the manor from the Earl of Derby.

As Thirsk's squire, Ralph lived in Thirsk Hall near St Mary's Church and the hall was evidently built in the 1720s, a project that may already have been underway when he acquired the manor.

Ralph died in 1735, whereupon the estate passed to a nephew who, in accord with his uncle's will, changed his surname to Bell. He, in turn, died in 1770 and was succeeded by a son named Ralph who soon engaged the services of John Carr of York, a prominent architect in the region, to enlarge the mansion. Consequently, the house was provided with an extra storey and lengthened by constructing two-storey wings.

At the other end of the social scale, in 1737 a workhouse capable of housing up to 40 destitute was founded in Thirsk and the inmates were required to undertake work, mostly spinning, in return for their food and lodging. The premises were located towards the northern end of Long Street on the northeast outskirts of the town.

Thirsk also had a modest spa close at hand. This was situated about half a mile to the north and lay beside the road to Northallerton. Lord Harley, the son of the Earl of Oxford, travelled past the spa in 1723 and, as the *Victoria History of the County of York* notes, wrote that it was 'covered by a thatched house, built by the Corporation, who have placed a poor old woman who makes what little profit she can from those who resort thither. It is said to have wrought many cures on lame and ricketty people.' The spa had three baths and was 'much frequented' at the beginning of the 19th century but no longer existed by 1859.

During the 18th century the appearance of Thirsk was gradually transformed, as was true of places elsewhere in Yorkshire such as Bedale and Richmond. Fine brick properties were constructed and timber-framed buildings therefore became increasingly outdated.

In the 1760s an attempt was made to boost Thirsk's economy by canalising the Cod Beck from the town to its junction with the River Swale, about six miles to the southwest. Parliament passed the neces-

Georgian houses in St James' Green

sary legislation in 1763 and work on the scheme, which included the proposed construction of five locks, began. However, the project was soon abandoned because of inadequate funds. Relics of this ill-fated venture include Canal Wharf (just south of Ingramgate) where barges would have loaded their cargoes if the project had come to fruition.

By the 1760s the Methodist movement, spearheaded by the zealous evangelical activity of John Wesley, who travelled extensively to preach the Word of God, had devotees in Thirsk which was on his itinerary from time to time. He first visited in 1747 after spending about six weeks on Tyneside and the surrounding area. He left Newcastle on 20 April, having preached in the Orphan House to some of the finest people he had ever seen, and arrived at Thirsk on the following day, Easter Monday. Here, to his dismay, the place was full of rowdy holiday folk, drinking, swearing, and enjoying the bloodthirsty sport of cock-fighting. He thus noted in his journal: 'I did not stop at all but rode on to Boroughbridge.' Wesley's 13th and final visit to the town occurred in 1788. His missionary work, as noted, bore fruit and from the mid 1760s the local Methodists worshipped in an octagonal chapel erected on St James' Green. The chapel survived into the early 19th century when it was demolished and replaced by a larger chapel in 1816.

Other denominations, of course, had a presence too. For instance, the Quakers rebuilt their meeting house in Kirkgate in 1799, and by 1804 the Independents had a chapel in Back Lane, today's Chapel Street. On the other hand, there was no place of worship for Catholics at this date and the nearest was situated at North Kilvington, approximately two miles away.

On 23 November 1755 Thomas Lord, who is best remembered as the founder of Lord's Cricket Ground, was born in a house in Kirkgate. But his days in Thirsk soon came to an end because the family moved to Norfolk where Thomas grew up. His birthplace still exists and houses Thirsk Museum which is run by volunteers and was established in 1975. Not surprisingly, exhibits in this small but delightful museum include cricketing memorabilia and one can also see a portrait of Thomas Lord which was presented by the MCC.

As in the past, fairs periodically enlivened the town. In 1751, for example, they were held on the Feasts of St James (25 July), St Luke (18 October) and St. Andrew (30 November), as well as on Shrove Monday and on the Tuesday after Lady Day.

Visitors, and people merely passing through, could find accommodation in substantial inns that sooner or later graced the Georgian town. One such was the Three Tuns, which still exists, and stands in the southwest corner of the Market Place. Evidently, some of the rear portions of the building date from the 17th century but the bulk of the structure is 18th-century and the interior is graced by an impressive staircase perhaps dating from the reign of Queen Anne (1702-14). Initially, the building is thought to have been the home of the lord of the manor until Thirsk Hall was erected in the 1720s. Its days as an inn are said to have begun in around 1740. It was run by the Cass family from 1773, who had previously operated an inn close at hand in today's Finkle Street. Notable guests at the Three Tuns included the poet William Wordsworth and his sister Dorothy, who stayed overnight in 1802.

The staircase of the Three Tuns

Rival businesses included the Golden Fleece, less than a stone's throw from the Three Tuns and likewise facing Market Place. Evidently, it too had once been a private residence and an attractive coffered ceiling in one of the rooms dates from the 17th century. In May 1810 the inn was acquired by an enterprising figure, George Blythe, and according to Will Swales a month later Blythe

> was able to advertise in several local newspapers that the Mail and Highflyer coaches to Newcastle and London called at The Golden Fleece, morning and evening, and that 'the Nobility, Gentry, Commercial Gentlemen and others will meet with such accommodations as cannot be surpassed on the road;' also that 'a constant supply of good Post Horses, convenient Chaises and careful Drivers may always be depended upon.'[1]

In the early 1820s, Blythe, who became a widower in 1822, increased the size of the premises. He died shortly thereafter, on 31 March 1828, having transformed the Golden Fleece into the town's premier coaching inn. The business was taken over by his niece and her husband, John Hall, who had already helped run the establishment for a number of years. Sadly, John went to an early grave in 1831 but his widow, Mary, continued to operate the concern. However, the business began to falter and by the time of her death in 1839, after a lengthy illness, some of the regular stage coaches no longer used the Golden Fleece. Following Mary's death the task of running the business was undertaken by two of her children, one of whom, William Hall, had been born in 1818.

The year 1821 witnessed the publication of Joseph Brown Jefferson's book, *History of Thirsk*. Jefferson describes the Market Place as 'a large square of noble dimensions, and consisting of many good houses, but unfortunately disfigured by some buildings in the centre.' Buildings here, located either side of an old market cross, included the timber-framed tollbooth which served, among other things, as the town hall and was located on the south side of the square. 'In the Toll Booth', states Jefferson, 'is conducted the business of the manor of Thirsk, by the appointed officers. The municipal government of the town, is

---

1   Incidentally, Blythe had married into the Cass family in 1795 and prior to purchasing the Golden Fleece, he and his wife had run an inn in Finkle Street.

vested in a bailiff, who is chosen by the burgage holders, and is sworn in by the steward of the Lord of the manor.'[1]

Bull-baiting occurred in the Market Place and a ring in the cobbles near the present bus stop reminds us of this bloody practice. The ill-fated bulls were tethered here and set upon by dogs. In addition to providing a spectacle for onlookers, it was thought that bull-baiting would improve the quality of the meat on the animal which, after the baiting, was led off to be slaughtered. Bull-baiting was subsequently made an offence by the Cruelty to Animals Act of 1835.[2]

Jefferson further comments: 'The town of Thirsk was formerly noted for the tanning business, and the manufactory of saddlery goods, particularly bridles, a considerable quantity of which were engaged for the army. These trades have declined of late years, particularly since the peace', i.e., the end of the Napoleonic Wars.

Of the bridges which spanned the Cod Beck, Jefferson observed:

> Were a stranger to travel over our bridges in the heat of summer, he might justly wonder at the size and number of the arches across so small a stream. But let him come this way at the time of a winter flood, and there will be abundant proof that they are not too large for the overflowing torrent pouring from the higher hills.[3]

Further information on Thirsk can be found in Pigot's *National Commercial Directory*, published in 1834. This says that the population at the time of the census in 1831 numbered 2,835, and that as 'a place of trade or manufactures, Thirsk does not take an elevated station; linen weaving is carried on to a limited extent, as are also brewing and malting, and there are some mills for grinding corn.'

Among other things, the directory records that the town's two breweries were located in Kirkgate, and that there were three china, glass and earthenware dealers, two of whom were located in the Market Place, where, moreover, one found the three inns, namely, the Crown, the

---

1   The tollbooth was destroyed by fire in 1834.

2   Although the main focus of commercial activity had long since moved to the Market Place, a cattle market continued to be held in St James' Green into the mid-19th century.

3   Indeed, from time to time the torrent of water gushing down the beck was of such volume that large-scale flooding occurred in the town, as was true for example in 1754, 1771 and 1826, and on more recent occasions too.

The Cross Keys in Kirkgate

Three Tuns and Golden Fleece. Some of the public houses mentioned are the Black Bull, the Black Lion, the Blacksmiths' Arms and the White Swan (all in the Market Place) and the Cross Keys in Kirkgate and the Lord Nelson in St James' Green.

Under the Great Reform Act of 1832, Thirsk became a one-member constituency—previously, as noted above, it had sent two MPs to parliament—and the constituency, which hitherto had merely comprised Old Thirsk (the part of the town on the east bank of the Cod Beck) was now greatly enlarged, so much so that Sowerby, Bagby, Carlton Miniott, Sandhutton and South Kilvington were henceforth part of the constituency.

At the general election held that year, Sir Robert Frankland was elected to represent Thirsk. The baronet was no stranger to the town. Indeed, he had served as one of Thirsk's MPs since 1815 (his family seat

was Thirkleby Hall, about four miles to the southeast) and his family were the largest landowners in the borough. Frankland was a Whig (moderate Liberal) and held the seat until he resigned from parliament in 1834.

Members of the Bell family, lords of the manor of Thirsk, also represented the parliamentary constituency. For instance, John Bell, who was born in 1809, became the MP for Thirsk in 1841. He was a Whig and was returned to parliament at the general election of 1847 but his mental health then took a turn for the worse. So much so, that a Commission of Lunacy was held in July 1849 and decided that he was insane. Nevertheless, he retained the seat until his death on 5 March 1851. His successor was the baronet, Sir William Payne-Gallwey, a Conservative who held the constituency until 1880 when he stood down. Sir William, who married one of the daughters of Sir Robert Frankland of Thirkleby Hall, died in 1881, aged 74, after sustaining severe internal injuries caused by falling upon a turnip while out hunting in the parish of Bagby. It was not until 1886 that parliament passed a law enabling members of unsound mind to be removed from their seats. Coincidentally, the parliamentary constituency of Thirsk had ceased to exist the previous year, for in 1885 it had been replaced by the constituency of Thirsk and Malton.

One of the major pieces of parliamentary legislation of the 19th century was the Poor Law Amendment Act of 1834. This resulted in the formation of the Thirsk Poor Law Union in February 1837, a body directed by a 41-strong Board of Guardians. The union not only cared for people at the bottom of society in Thirsk and neighbouring communities such as Carlton Miniott and Sowerby, but over a wide ranging area that included far-flung places such as Boltby, Newby Wiske, Kilburn and Topcliffe.

The Board of Guardians soon concluded that the existing workhouses were unsuitable and ordered the construction of a large replacement on Sutton Road (on the southeast fringe of Thirsk) and the building was completed in January 1839. The facilities were subsequently enlarged and in 1886 a hospital for infectious cases was constructed in the grounds. Of the workhouse, Peter Higginbotham comments: 'Thirsk

Opposite: The former workhouse

gained a reputation for being one of the best managed workhouses in the north, mostly due to the influence of the Guardians' vice-chairman, Thomas Smith, a local draper and grocer, and a Quaker. Work given to male inmates included stone-breaking, and the grinding of corn using a handmill. Women performed domestic work or picked oakum.' In addition, in 1847 Thirsk Poor Law Union was one of the first to appoint proper teachers as members of staff. The workhouse survived until 1930 when, under legislation passed the previous year, Poor Law Unions were abolished nationwide and the buildings passed into the hands of the County Council and were mostly disused for several years. They were then used as part of the war effort during the Second World War and later housed a furniture factory. The former infirmary was demolished in the late 1990s but the main block survives and has been converted into flats.

In the Victorian era there were several schools in the town and *Whellan's Directory* of 1859 notes:

> The British School in the old town, is a large commodious building of brick, with a house for the master, erected in 1841. This school, which is supported by subscription, is attended by about 200 children of both sexes. The Infant School, near the York Bridge, is held in a suitable building, adjoining which is a house for the school mistress. About 70 or 80 children usually attend this school,

which is likewise supported by subscription. In the Castle Yard is the Charity School for 31 girls, who are taught reading, writing, knitting and sewing. It too is aided by voluntary subscription.[1]

Adults eager to enhance their knowledge could benefit from attending the Mechanics' Institute. Such institutes had been founded nation-wide since the early 1820s to serve as places of education and relaxation for working men. Thirsk's Mechanics' Institute was established in 1846 (earlier than is sometimes said) and was initially housed in rented accommodation in Back Lane. The institute struck a favourable chord. Hence at a meeting on 5 June 1851, the members informed their president, Sir William Payne-Gallwey, Thirsk's MP, that more suitable accommodation was required. He thus constructed premises on the corner of Westgate. These opened on 2 January 1852 and were leased from Payne-Gallwey. Of the institute, J. Popple has commented: 'To supplement their library, for some time the only public one in town, books were hired from Mudie's Library, London, but this experiment of 1866-7 was not sufficiently successful to continue.' Popple further notes that from the mid 1870s the institute only leased part of the premises and that financial problems forced them to sell their piano in 1882. Shortly thereafter, on 1 January 1884, the institute amalgamated with the Thirsk Church Institute (formed in 1877) to become the Thirsk Institute, using rooms in the premises built on Westgate over 30 years earlier.

Religion, of course, continued to play an important role in the lives of some of Thirsk's inhabitants and denominations included the Independents, who moved to a new chapel built on Finkle Street in 1845; a chapel that soon needed to be rebuilt because of the inadequate quality of construction. For their part, the Primitive Methodists erected a substantial chapel in Castlegate (the foundation stone was laid on 5 November 1851 and the opening services were held on 6 June 1852) and, in 1867, the Catholics likewise constructed a large place of worship, All Saints, on the opposite side of the same thoroughfare.

A member of the town's Quaker community was the draper and botanist, John Gilbert Baker, whose book *North Yorkshire, studies of its*

---

1   The abovementioned Infants' School dated from 1833 and was erected on Finkle Street. The building still exists but is no longer a school.

botany, geology, climate and physical geography was published in 1863. Although not a native of the town, he was nonetheless a Yorkshireman for he was born in Guisborough in 1834.

Baker, who married a fellow Quaker on Tyneside in 1860, lived and worked in premises on the west side of the Market Place and a blue plaque in Baker's Alley marks the site. Sadly, on 10 May 1864 the premises went up in flames and of this event the *York Herald* commented on 22 October:

> In May last, the business premises and adjoining dwelling-houses of Mr. J. G. Baker and his brother, at Thirsk, were utterly destroyed by fire, the two families barely escaping with their lives, whilst the whole scientific library and herbarium of Mr. Baker became prey of the rapid conflagration. The amount of insurance being small in comparison with the value of the property destroyed, it might have been a long time ere Mr. Baker could have replaced his lost books. This fact becoming known, his scientific friends have raised a subscription, which, we are glad to learn, has been found more than sufficient for replacing the lost books.

After the fire, Baker briefly resided in Sussex before taking up a post at the herbarium at the renowned Kew Gardens in 1866. On the other hand, the gutted premises in Thirsk were replaced by an imposing building that now houses the Thirsk branch of NatWest Bank.[1]

By this time the people of Thirsk were well acquainted with travel by rail, for on 31 March 1841 the Great North of England Railway Company had opened a station about a mile to the west of the town; a station located on a line that was being laid to run between York and Newcastle—authorisation for the railway was granted in 1837, coincidentally the year Queen Victoria ascended the throne. In 1848, moreover, a newer concern, the Leeds & Thirsk Railway, opened a station on the western fringe of Thirsk's town centre—the site is now occupied by a Tesco Superstore. Minerals were conveyed along the line from 5 January onward, and on 1 June of the same year a passenger service likewise commenced. The latter service, though, was not a

---

1   Although Baker died at Kew in 1920, he was interred in the burial ground attached to the Quaker meeting house in Thirsk.

success and evidently ceased at the end of 1855 but freight continued to be transported into the second half of the 1960s.

Railways inevitably had a detrimental effect on stage coaches and coaching inns such as the Golden Fleece which was run in the Victorian era by William Hall. In the opening years of the 20th century Edmund Bogg wrote evocatively about the inn before coaching was eclipsed by rail:

> Mr Hall generally kept upwards of fifty horses in his possession for coaching purposes. How silent is this old inn yard to-day compared with the activity displayed in the past; the hurry and scurry and running hither and thither of the groom and the stable-man; the rattling of wheels and clattering of hoofs and fiery sparks flying from the cobbled pavement; hark to the sounding horn and crack of the coachman's whip.

Nevertheless, despite the marked downturn in travel by stage coach, Hall continued to trade successfully. Of him, Swales thus comments:

> He maintained the stables, and established a good trade in hiring horses and carriages. He made his establishment a leading venue for the functions of various social organisations of the great and the good, which invariably included him as a member. Even at dinners held at other venues it appears that William Hall was the preferred choice of outside caterer.

What is more, in addition to running the inn, which he renamed Hall's Fleece Hotel, he bought a farm to the east of Thirsk and granted land on the town's outskirts to serve as a cricket ground and the first match was played in 1851.

Hall was also involved in the commencement of horseracing at Thirsk, which began on a modest scale on 15 March 1855 after a meeting at the Golden Fleece and he served on the first racecourse committee. Races took place on the western margins of the town where the lord of the manor, Frederick Bell, set up a rudimentary course. From 1875, however, thanks to the efforts of the clerk of the course, Thomas Dawson junior, Thirsk's importance as a racing venue increased as prize money rose and riders and mounts came from further afield. Furthermore, on 17 and 18 October 1895 Queen Victoria's eldest son (the future Edward VII) attended the races and the Royal Pavilion was erected for the visit of the prince and his entourage.

During the Victorian era a well-established mill operated beside the Cod Beck. Rymer's Mill was situated on the west bank of the stream and on a wedge of land immediately to the south of Bridge Street and was a substantial brick structure of three storeys—several stone courses incorporated low in the east wall likely belonged to a supposed earlier mill. Rymer's machinery included two water-powered wheels within the building. These powered millstones that ground cereals into flour and output also included animal feed.

A regular supply of water for the mill was provided by erecting a weir to dam the Cod Beck about a quarter of a mile upstream. There, a sluice gate controlled the supply of water that was diverted from the dammed beck and channelled along a mill race. For part of its length, the channel was located beside the Northallerton Road, before proceeding in a southeasterly direction towards the mill. Hence, as a display board comments: 'The miller was therefore not dependent on the vagaries of the supply from the river; he could control when and

The weir

how much water he required to undertake his milling.' The technology at Rymer's was updated in 1855 when a boiler house and chimney were erected and a steam engine was installed. In time, this was superseded by an oil engine.

Basket making was undertaken at Norby in the Victorian period and willows, to provide the raw material, were grown profusely along the banks of the Cod Beck. On an annual basis the trees were cut to encourage the growth of new slender shoots suitable for making baskets.

Turning to other matters, in 1857 the Frankland family constructed one of Thirsk's most noteworthy buildings, Fox Wynd, on the north side of Ingramgate. Designed by Edward Lamb, it was built to house employees of Lady Frankland-Russell of Thirkleby and is in the English Revival Style. From the 1850s onward, moreover, a number of streets and villas were constructed on the southwest outskirts of the town, thereby linking Thirsk with neighbouring Sowerby which was beginning to be viewed as a suburb.

One of the people associated with Sowerby was Thirsk's most well-known businessman, Adam Carlisle Bamlett, who was born in the North East in 1835 and moved to Thirsk in 1860 where he began small-scale production of agricultural implements in premises on Station Road. Of his horse-drawn mower, Cooper Harding aptly comments that it was 'efficient, reliable and cheap enough for the small farmer to buy, [and] was exported all over the world.' Of Bamlett, the journal of the Institute of Mechanical Engineers noted in 1912: 'By dint of continual experimenting, he so improved the construction of his various products that the business rapidly increased both at home and abroad, and he was rewarded with the success of his machines in competition at Agricultural Meetings and by the award of various medals at the Paris Exhibitions of 1878 and 1889 and at other exhibitions.'[1]

By 1912 the Lambert Memorial Hospital, in Chapel Street, was a well-established institution in Thirsk. It opened in September 1890

---

1   Such was Bamlett's success that he became Thirsk's largest employer. Like many other successful businessmen, he also played a role in local government. He was, for instance, a long-serving member of Thirsk Rural District Council (formed in 1894) and was chairman of Sowerby Parish Council. He died at his home in Sowerby in January 1912, after suffering prolonged bad health.

Fox Wynd

and was endowed by a wealthy widow, Sarah Lambert, who lived in Sowerby. She had married a local doctor who died from tuberculosis in 1853 and the couple's son likewise died at a young age from the same ailment. Consequently, after Sarah inherited a fortune from an uncle in Manchester in the mid 1880s, she devoted the money to charitable causes, most notably by founding the Lambert Memorial Hospital.

In the closing decade of the Victorian era the centre of Thirsk was enhanced by the construction of the market clock, incorporating a drinking fountain. It was built to commemorate the marriage of the Duke of York to Princess Mary of Teck. The couple married in 1893 but the attractive memorial—which replaced the remnants of an old market cross—was only completed three years later and is still a cherished landmark.

FROM THE EDWARDIAN
ERA TO THE PRESENT

At the beginning of the 20th century one of the notable figures in Thirsk was William Welbank Hall, the proprietor of the Fleece Hotel, a business his father (also named William) had run for much of the previous century. The hotel had a good reputation and thus continued to attract well-heeled clientele. That was certainly the case in the summer of 1911 when Thirsk was on the route of a motorcar rally in which members of high society (including Prince Henry of Prussia, a member of the German Royal Family) were participants. As such, on 12 July, Hall and his staff provided luncheon to the prince and his fellow contestants.[1]

The lively and exhilarating rally was a far cry from the dark days that lay ahead when the Great War broke out in August 1914, a conflict that inevitably profoundly affected the lives of the people of Thirsk and saw a large proportion of the town's menfolk heading off to fight in France and elsewhere. Consequently, women took on new roles. For instance, some joined the workforce of Bamlett's and the company's output included products for the war effort. Women, of course, comprised much of the staff at the Lambert Memorial Hospital—which had been extended by public subscription in 1906—and some patients were wounded servicemen brought to Thirsk from the horrendous battlefields of the Great War; and other wounded members of the armed forces were treated at the Town Hall (built in 1913) which was converted into a convalescent hospital. The war ended in November 1918 and the following year Thirsk held a Victory Parade to celebrate peace and to remember the fallen.[2]

During the depressing war years some people found solace by attending the town's cinema, the Picture House, which had opened

1   Hall sold the business in 1918 and it reverted to its former name, the Golden Fleece.
2   On 29 May 1921 a memorial service was held in St Mary's Church to honour the men of Thirsk who had died in the war. The numerous fatalities included 20-year-old Private Henry Dodsworth, killed in action on 24 April 1915, and 26-year-old Sergeant Herbert Beadle who had died of wounds in France on 25 June 1917.

A postcard of 1904 showing the mill race and parish church

in March 1912. This was the brainchild of a local man, Walter Power, who converted the premises erected in Victorian times for the town's Mechanics' Institute into a suitable venue to show films. Many residents of Thirsk and the neighbouring villages enjoyed whiling away some of their leisure time in the cinema, a welcome addition to places of entertainment.

As the 1920s drew to a close, seating capacity at the cinema was increased and it was renamed the Ritz. In addition, silent movies were replaced by the first 'talkies.' Other events that occurred in the inter-war years included the opening of Thirsk's first secondary school in 1920 on Topcliffe Road and the co-educational school originally had around 120 pupils,[1] whereas in the years 1925-6 the Thirsk and Sowerby Institute (extant since 1842) erected new premises on the southern fringe of the town. In 1930 it was noted that the facilities comprised, among other things, a room containing four full-size billiard tables, a general

---

1   In 1957 the school moved to premises further down Topcliffe Road and Sowerby Community Primary School now occupies the original site.

reading room, and a library with over 1,500 volumes. What is more, in the grounds were two recent hard tennis courts.

The above information on the institute is taken from a handbook entitled *Thirsk Shopping Week, May 31st to June 7th 1930* in which a 'business crusade' was promoted to encourage the townsfolk to support local enterprise. The introduction states:

> Encouraged by the splendid support given to their last year's effort, the Thirsk Chamber of Trade are again making an attempt to increase, and improve, local business, by organising a SECOND SHOPPING WEEK....Prosperity in our town is essential if Thirsk is to maintain the happy position she has held in the past....The Chamber of Trade realise that owing to the growth of Mail Ordering and increased transport facilities, competition is greater than at any previous period of the town's history, but it is confident that Members can give as good value and service in their respective callings as can be obtained anywhere else, and apart from other considerations advantages are to be gained by knowing the people with whom you do business, especially when their interests centre on one's own 'Home Town.'

Businesses with advertisements in the handbook included W. Bennett, which was located in Millgate and strongly recommended the purchase of K shoes; William Foggitt and Sons, Chemists, in the Market Place;

and the Electric Shop in Kirkgate run by Eric Thompson, an 'Electrical Engineer and Wireless Specialist.'[1]

The handbook also mentions Thirsk Golf Club and several other clubs. Of the former, we read:

> The Thirsk Golf Links are situated about a mile from the town on the Northallerton Road, in an ideal position, with magnificent views of the surrounding hills. The course is as good as any inland course could be, and the Committee are carrying out improvements to induce a larger membership.[2]

The handbook also states that Thirsk Swimming Club

> has taken advantage of a natural pool located at a corner of the Cod beck above the Town, to make a place suitable for bathing and swimming. Dressing cubicles have been erected, and improvements made, calculated to attract more members to avail themselves of the accommodation offered. Facilities are offered for those boys and girls who wish to learn to swim.[3]

When the handbook was published the Depression had recently begun and this international recession undoubtedly affected the lives of the people of Thirsk. However, the places worst hit were major industrial centres such as the shipbuilding town of Jarrow on Tyneside. So bad did the situation become there that on Monday, 5 October 1936, unemployed workers began marching towards London to highlight their town's plight. An itinerary of the planned route states that the marchers would travel through Thirsk and arrive in the town on Friday the 9th. But this did not occur for a change of plan ensued and they headed towards Ripon instead.

---

1   Foggitt's was a well-established firm. It dated from 1836 and was taken over by Boots in the mid 1930s. On the other hand, Eric Thompson founded his business in 1923 and the highly regarded shop survived until 2014, by which time it was run by David and Susan Higgs. Incidentally, Thompson was very interested in local history and wrote *My Book of Thirsk*, which was published in 1947 and contains much useful information.

2   The Golf Club was founded in 1914 and subsequently changed its name to the Thirsk & Northallerton Golf Club in 1949. Initially, the course had 9 holes but there have been 18 since 1997.

3   The club had officially been opened on Tuesday, 16 August 1910 by Reginald Bell of Thirsk Hall. Sometimes, of course, the beck was far from a blessing. For example, on 23 July 1930, following torrential rain, it caused severe flooding in Finkle Street and others parts of town.

On 3 September 1939 Great Britain declared war on Nazi Germany (in response to Hitler's invasion of Poland two days earlier) and as a result petrol and various items of food were soon rationed. Locally, additional measures which resulted from the onset of war included erecting concrete barriers in the Market Place in order to hinder the movement of German tanks if an invasion occurred; and the turning of Thirsk Racecourse into an army camp.

Plans to evacuate children from danger zones in the event of war were promptly put into effect. Consequently, evacuees were billeted in the town and surrounding villages. On 25 September 1939 Thirsk Rural District Council was informed by the local evacuation officer that 1,376 people had arrived, including teachers and mothers accompanying very young children. Indeed, the first evacuees had come on 1 September and comprised 712 youngsters from Gateshead whereas on 3 September 452 children came from Sunderland. The newcomers arrived by train and were fed at Thirsk Racecourse before being allocated to homes. In addition, other evacuees from Gateshead arrived in July 1940.

Many evacuees soon returned home but Annie Anderson (from Gateshead) was not one of them. In fact, she spent two years in Thirsk and was present when a solitary German bomber caused death and destruction on the evening of 16 October 1940. Of the event, she recalls:

> One night we heard the drone of a German plane overhead and the next minute there was an almighty bang and all of the cottage windows blew out!! A neighbour was cutting my hair at the time and she ran out screaming and left me with lopsided hair! The bomb had dropped on the school just on the other side of Long Street and completely demolished our classroom.

Bombs from the same aircraft fell over a wide area, including the army camp at the racecourse. In all, 106 houses were slightly damaged. Another 36 were more seriously affected but were deemed useable, whereas two properties had to be evacuated.

Crashing planes added to the danger. For instance, on the afternoon of 11 July 1942 a Halifax bomber, taking part in a training exercise from the airbase at Topcliffe, crashed in Station Road. Four of the crew sustained minor injuries, as did a civilian walking along the road, but no one was killed. Moreover, four houses were damaged, including the home of the Severs family (number 49) which was deemed beyond repair. A much more serious incident occurred just over a month later, on 18 August 1942, when a Halifax from Middleton St George plummeted into Green Lane, Sowerby, killing all seven aircrew. Furthermore, in poor weather late on 15 April 1944 another Halifax, based at Dishforth, crashed with fatal results. It came down on the Railway Cottages, near the railway bridge on Topcliffe Road, killing five of the crew and two residents, as well as a farm labourer cycling home from the pub. Sadly, these were not the only fatal incidents involving aircraft that came to grief in and around the town.

On a much lighter note, the presence of a large number of military personnel in the neighbourhood, many of whom were from Canada, enlivened Thirsk's social scene. Among venues that benefited were the Ritz (recently acquired from the late Walter Power's family by the Schofields of Leeds) and the town's other cinema, the Regent, which had opened in 1935 and could seat 400.

A memorial at the site in Skipton-on-Swale where a Halifax bomber crashed in 1944

In 1948, three years after the war ended, the Lambert Memorial Hospital passed into the hands of the National Health Service, created that year, and was given a thorough overhaul which included redecorating and re-equipping the premises, improving staffing, and providing mobile X-ray apparatus.[1] What is more, in the early 1950s an adjacent property, 2 Chapel Street, was purchased in order to expand the facilities.

In the same decade, measures were taken to improve the quality of housing in rundown parts of Thirsk. This had a dramatic effect on Norby. Of redevelopment here, a report noted in 1957:

> The first major step in the post-war drive to deal with the bad housing conditions in the district was made possible by the progress on the Norby Housing Site. The whole of the Norby area was surveyed, and every house inspected. 49 houses were found unfit, largely because of lack of amenities, dampness and bad arrangement on site. From the results of this survey the Council decided that the best method of dealing with the conditions in the area north of the Public House was by the demolition of all the buildings in the area.

Some of the debris from the dwellings pulled down in Norby was used to fill in the mill race of Rymer's Mill (a business that had continued to operate into the post-war era) and the demolished properties were replaced by council houses. Hence the 1959 annual report of the Public Health Inspector for Thirsk Rural District Council states that 36 new dwellings had been completed at Norby.[2]

The annual report for 1959 also comments:

> Thirsk appears to be a favourite stopping place for long-distance coach parties, and one suspects that, even allowing for the natural charm of the place, its comparatively modern public lavatories are also something of an attraction. Some 160,738 people passed through the turnstiles in 1959.

By the late 60s, increasing traffic congestion was becoming a problem

---

1   Upon the establishment of the NHS, Thirsk's hospital came under the York 'A' Group Hospital Management Committee, a state of affairs that lasted until 1974 when the Lambert Memorial Hospital was transferred to the Northallerton Health District.

2   The total number of council houses in Thirsk and its environs now stood at 616 whereas in 1939 there had only been 149.

for the number of vehicles plying the roads was rapidly growing. This state of affairs was mitigated by major road construction which occurred in the vicinity and resulted in the opening of the A19 bypass in 1972. Hence, the volume of lorries and other vehicles passing through the town fell dramatically, a welcome development for many of the locals.

In 1968 Scottish and Newcastle Breweries hoped to sell the Three Tuns to a London property developer who wished to demolish the historic structure and replace it with a shopping centre, but fortunately this idea did not come to fruition. One of Thirsk's most historic buildings thus still graces the town centre and today the hotel is one of over 50 operated nationwide by Wetherspoons and its chief local rival is the Golden Fleece, now part of the Coaching Inn Group.

Some visitors to Thirsk are attracted to the town because of its connection with the famous author, James Herriot, whose real name was James Alfred Wight. Alf (as he was informally known) was born in Sunderland on 3 October 1916 but grew up in Glasgow where he studied veterinary medicine. In 1940, soon after qualifying, he moved to Thirsk—after a brief return to Sunderland—and joined a practice in

The Golden Fleece by night

23 Kirkgate. Moreover, just over a year later, on 5 November 1941, he married a local secretary, Joan Danbury, and the wedding took place in the parish church, little more than a stone's throw from the surgery.

In 1966, at the urging of his wife, Alf (who had long desired to be a writer) finally put pen to paper. Sadly, his material, which included stories on football, a theme dear to his heart for he was a lifelong supporter of Sunderland AFC, was rejected by publishers. But, undaunted, he persevered and in 1969, using the pen name James Herriot, wrote *If Only They Could Talk*, the first in a series of semi-auto-biographical works partly highlighting the humorous and sometimes challenging situations encountered by members of the veterinary profession. The book was published in England in 1970 but sales were modest. However, in 1972 an American firm published *All Creatures Great and Small*—a volume that combined *If Only They Could Talk* with Wight's second novel, *It Shouldn't Happen to a Vet*—and this proved a great success. Consequently, Alf's adopted hometown found itself in the limelight as the home of a prominent and much-loved author. Furthermore, a film entitled *All Creatures Great and Small* appeared in 1975 and a very popular TV series with the same name was first aired in January 1978 and ran for many years.[1]

Despite his international fame, Alf Wight continued to live locally and work as a vet and one of his colleagues was his son, Jim, who had joined the practice in 1966. Eventually, Alf moved to the village of Thirlby (about four miles east of Thirsk) where he died on 23 February 1995 after battling cancer.

Shortly afterwards, on 4 March 1995 the Ritz Cinema, which had recently closed, reopened partly thanks to the assistance of Thirsk Town Council. It did so as a community cinema run by volunteers. On the other hand, the Regent had ceased to be a cinema in the early 1970s when it had become a bingo hall, a role it retained until the summer of 2005 and the building was demolished the following year.

In 2011, the year of the most recent national census, Thirsk had a population of 4,998 and the figure for neighbouring Sowerby was 4,249. The census returns also show that Thirsk and Sowerby are much

---

1   The film and TV series were shot elsewhere in Yorkshire, namely Ryedale for the film and upper Wensleydale for the TV series.

less ethnically diverse than many other places in the country, for 98.1 per cent of the residents of Thirsk were white and the figure for Sowerby was 98.2 per cent.

Turning to other matters, in 2015 the 14-bed Lambert Memorial Hospital was closed by the South Tees NHS Hospital Trust, a move which aroused strong local opposition. The closure was a temporary measure but the following year it was decided to close the hospital permanently and it now survives merely as an outpatient centre for physiotherapy.

Thirsk's retail sector inevitably includes branches of international chains, such as Boots, Tesco and Lidl. As noted earlier, Boots arrived in the mid 1930s but the current premises (on the same site) were erected in the 1960s. Tesco's presence dates from September 1994 when it took over a supermarket built on Station Road in the late 1980s by W.M. Low, a retail chain based in Scotland. Tesco's in Thirsk is now a super-store and by far the largest retail outlet in the town. Little more than

White Rose Book Café alongside the Blacksmiths Arms

a stone's throw from the shop, one finds Lidl, a low-budget rival that opened in July 2009.

Noteworthy independent businesses include the Well-Heeled Boutique and Venture Cycles. The former specialises in good quality women's wear and was founded by Jane Jackson in August 2010, and has been at its current location in the Market Place since July 2013. Venture Cycles, likewise in the Market Place, opened in May 2014 and was founded by Iaen Bell who has presumably benefited from the recent upsurge in interest in cycling, partly as a result of high profile long distance races such as the Tour de Yorkshire which have featured Thirsk as part of their route.

One of Thirsk's most well-known independent businesses is the White Rose Book Café. The bookshop opened in October 1995 and the founders were Steve Clements and his daughter, Sue. The premises now also house a large café—an addition to the business and a feature which greatly enhances a visit to the bookshop, whose facilities also include a garden.

Booklovers, of course, also benefit from the existence of Thirsk Community Library. Since August 2015 this has been located in Meadowfields, Chapel Street. The library has larger and brighter premises than was true at its previous location, the former Infants' School on Finkle Street, and has been run by volunteers since 1 April 2017.

Meadowfields also contains over 50 self-contained apartments for the elderly who are supported by an on-site care team and the housing project was officially opened in December 2015. Furthermore, recent decades have witnessed the construction of numerous houses, including substantial detached properties on Stockton Road and elsewhere.

Thirsk is a vibrant and attractive town and has much to offer visitors and locals alike. Furthermore, its proximity to the North York Moors and Yorkshire Dales greatly enhances its appeal to would-be residents and anyone contemplating a holiday in the Vale of Mowbray.

BIBLIOGRAPHY

Adamson, D., *Union Workhouse, Thirsk*, 2001.

Burton, E., *The Foundation History of the Abbeys of Byland and Jervaulx*, 2006.

Gillingham, J., 'Two Yorkshire Historians Compared: Roger of Howden and William of Newburgh', in S. Morillo (ed.), *The Haskins Society Journal – Studies in Medieval History* volume 12, 2002.

Harding, C., *Thirsk & Sowerby from Old Photographs, a Second Selection*, 2011.

Harding, C. & Wyon, P., *Britain in Old Photographs: Around Thirsk*, 1995.

Higginbotham, P., *The Workhouse in Thirsk, Yorkshire, North Riding*.

Jefferson, J.B., *The History of Thirsk*, 1821.

Masinton, A., Sacred Space: Priorities, Perception and the Presence of God in Late Medieval Yorkshire Parish Churches, volumes 1 and 2, 2006. (PhD thesis).

Moore, G., *Thirsk at War 1939-1945*, 2004.

Pevsner, N., *The Buildings of England – Yorkshire: the North Riding*, 1966.

Poole, G.A., *Churches of Yorkshire, volume 1*, 1844.

Popple, J., 'The Mechanics' Institutes of the East and North Ridings and of York, 1837-1887', in *The Vocational Aspect of Secondary and Further Education*, 1958.

Roberts, H. E., *Researching Yorkshire Quaker History – a guide to sources*, 2003 (updated 2007).

Swales, W., *The Golden Fleece, Hotel, Eatery & Coffee House, A Brief History*, 2016.

Trotter, E., *Seventeenth Century Life in the Country Parish, with special reference to Local Government*, 1919.

Webb, K. A., *From County Hospital to NHS Trust, the history and archives of NHS hospitals, services and management in York 1740-2000, volume 1*, 2002.

Weston, M., 'Thirsk' in W. Page (ed.), *Victoria History of the County of York: North Riding, volume 2*, 1923.

Woods, J., 'Quakers in Thirsk Monthly Meeting 1650-75', *Quaker Studies*, vol. 9, 2005.

OF RELATED INTEREST

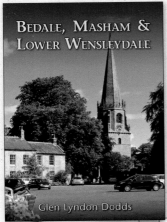

Bedale, Masham & Lower Wensleydale
Glen Lyndon Dodds

ISBN 978 0 9932527 1 6

Available in both softback (56pp) and Kindle formats at Amazon.co.uk

Albion Press
40 Park Parade Roker Sunderland Tyne & Wear
© Glen Lyndon Dodds 2019. Reprinted 2022

ISBN 978 0 9932527 8 5

For more information on Albion Press titles email albionpress@gmail.com

Typeset and designed by UpStyle Book Design
www.upstyledesign.co.uk

Printed and bound in Great Britain by
Mixam UK Ltd., 6 Hercules Way, Watford, Hertfordshire WD25 7GS